Meet my neighbor, the dentist

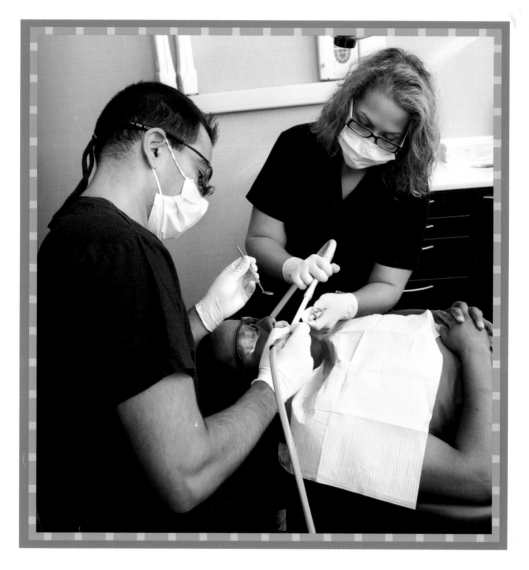

Marc Crabtree

Author and Photographer

Crabtree Publishing Company

www.crabtreebooks.com

🌴 Crabtree Publishing Company

Meet my neighbor, the dentist

For David and Hila, with thanks

Author and photographer
Marc Crabtree

Editor
Reagan Miller

Proofreaders
Corey Long
Crystal Sikkens

Design
Samantha Crabtree

Production coordinator
Margaret Amy Salter

Photographs
All photographs by Marc Crabtree except:
Shutterstock: pages 3, 24 (except patient and
dental tools)

Library and Archives Canada Cataloguing in Publication

Crabtree, Marc
    Meet my neighbor, the dentist / Marc Crabtree, author and
photographer.

(Meet my neighbor)
ISBN 978-0-7787-4573-0 (bound).--ISBN 978-0-7787-4583-9 (pbk.)

    1. Meisels, David, 1967- --Juvenile literature. 2. Dentists--Canada--
Biography--Juvenile literature. 3. Dentistry--Juvenile literature. I. Title.
II. Series: Crabtree, Marc. Meet my neighbor.

RK43.M43C73 2010   j617.6092   C2009-906758-7

Library of Congress Cataloging-in-Publication Data

Crabtree, Marc.
 Meet my neighbor, the dentist / author and photographer, Marc
Crabtree.
    p. cm.
ISBN 978-0-7787-4573-0 (reinforced lib. bdg. : alk. paper) --
ISBN 978-0-7787-4583-9 (pbk. : alk. paper)
1. Dentistry--Juvenile literature. 2. Dentists--Juvenile literature.
I. Title.

RK60.C73 2010
617.6--dc22

                                        2009046547

Crabtree Publishing Company

www.crabtreebooks.com   1-800-387-7650

Printed in the USA/122009/CG20091120

Published in Canada
Crabtree Publishing
616 Welland Ave.
St. Catharines, Ontario
L2M 5V6

Published in the United States
Crabtree Publishing
PMB 59051
350 Fifth Avenue, 59th Floor
New York, New York 10118

Published in the United Kingdom
Crabtree Publishing
Maritime House
Basin Road North, Hove
BN41 1WR

Published in Australia
Crabtree Publishing
386 Mt. Alexander Rd.
Ascot Vale (Melbourne)
VIC 3032

Contents

Meet my Neighbor

Meet my neighbor, Doctor David Meisels, the dentist.

David is at home with his wife, Hila, and their daughters, Brit and Shiraz.

Brit and Shiraz help their parents make strawberry pancakes for breakfast.

At his office, David washes his hands before treating his **patient**, Jacqueline. He also puts on gloves.

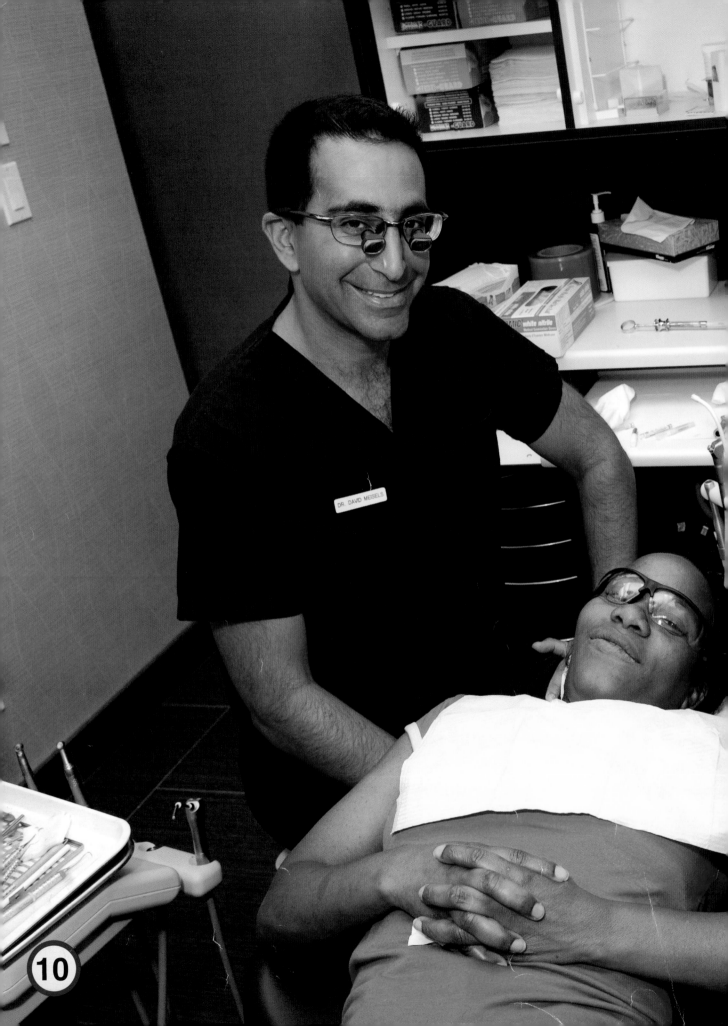

David and his assistant, Chantel, are going to clean Jacqueline's teeth and fill a **cavity**. This is the dental care Jacqueline needs to keep her mouth healthy.

David and Chantel look at a picture of Jacqueline's teeth called an **X-ray**.

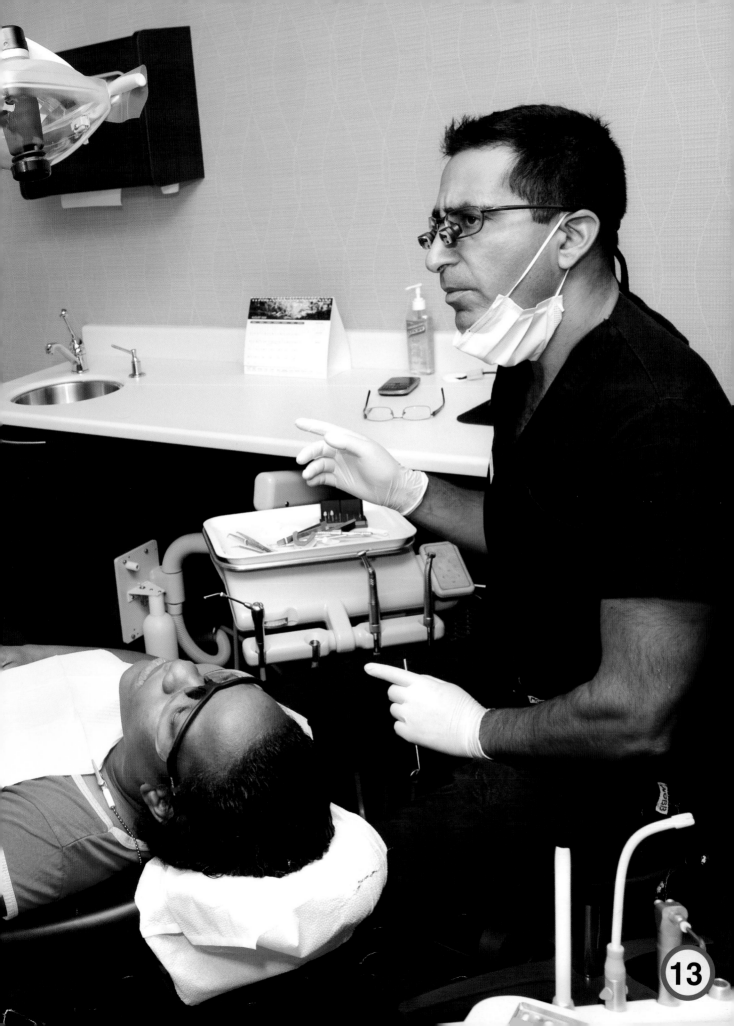

13

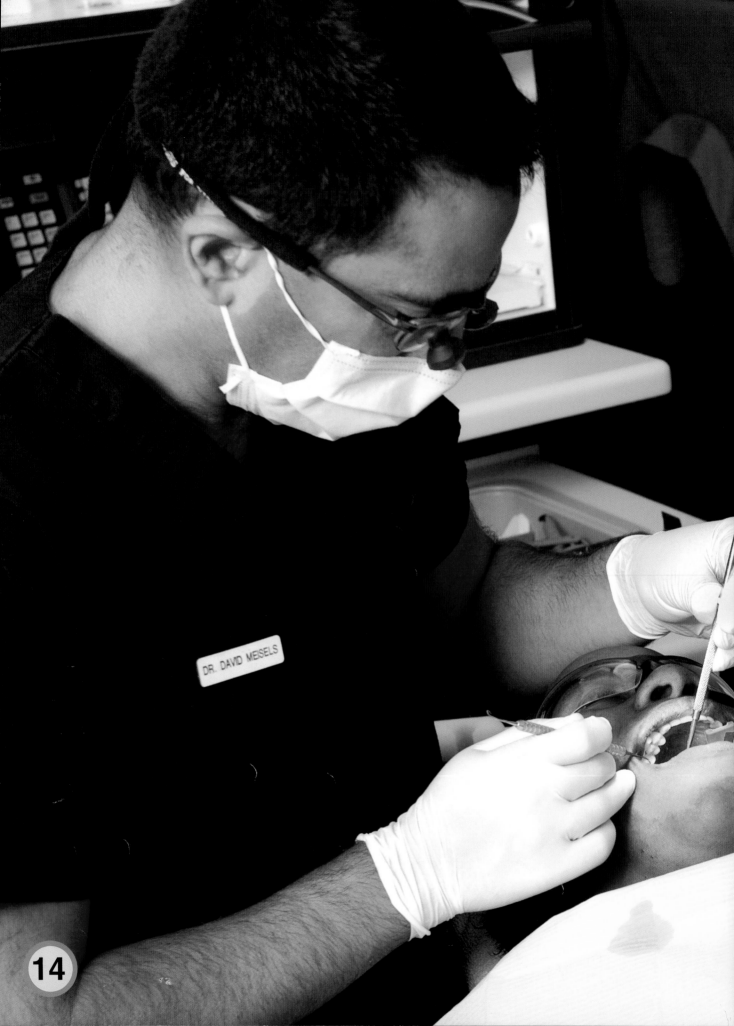

David and Chantel
are cleaning
Jacqueline's teeth.

David wears special glasses so he can see Jacqueline's teeth up close.

David is finished cleaning Jacqueline's teeth. She rinses her mouth with water.

Next, Chantel helps David fill a cavity in Jacqueline's tooth.

David uses his tools to fill the cavity.

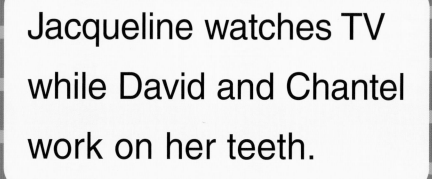

Jacqueline watches TV while David and Chantel work on her teeth.

Chantel shows Jacqueline how to clean her teeth using **dental floss**.

Jacqueline's appointment is done. Chantel cleans the **dental tools**.

Chantel puts the dental tools away in the cupboard until the next patient arrives.

Jacqueline is happy with her clean, healthy teeth. Christina, the receptionist, books Jacqueline's next appointment.

David finds out who the next patient he will help is.

Glossary

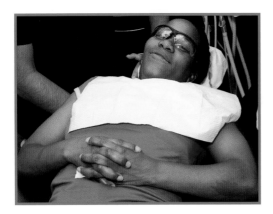

patient

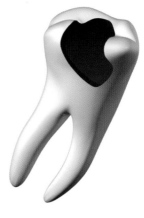

cavity

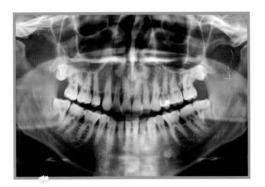

X-ray

dental floss

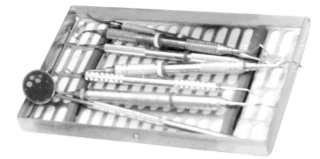

dental tools

Printed in the U.S.A. - CG